Hey Everybody . . .

By teaming up with New Leaf Paper Company and printing *All the Way to the Ocean*
using their Primavera Gloss (made from 80% recycled fiber, of which 60% is post-consumer
waste, elemental chlorine free and the remaining 20% from FSC certified virgin fiber),
we were able to help protect the environment and save the following natural resources:

- ✔ 15,194 gallons of water
- ✔ 33 full grown trees
- ✔ 922 pounds of solid waste
- ✔ 3,155 pounds of greenhouse gases
- ✔ 11 million BTUs of energy

See how easy it is when we all work together!
We even used soy ink. Soy ink is less harmful to the
environment by producing less airborne toxins than
regular ink. Log on and learn about ways you and your
friends can make a difference: www.sosforkids.com

Isaac

James

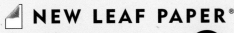

NEW LEAF PAPER®

NEW LEAF PAPER
manufactured with **wind power**

FSC Mixed Sources
Product group from well-managed
forests, controlled sources and
recycled wood or fiber
www.fsc.org Cert no. BV-COC-930557
© 1996 Forest Stewardship Council

PRINTED WITH
SOY INK™

Published by

Freedom Three Publishing

FREEDOM

THREE

310 N. Indian Hill Blvd. #442, Claremont, CA 91711
www.freedomthree.com

ISBN 0-9714254-1-8
Library of Congress Control Number: 2005907280

All the Way to the Ocean was illustrated primarily with Prismacolor pencils on bristol board. Book design by Marq Spusta. Production assistant Dustin Lawson, DustinLawson.com

Printed in the U.S.A. by Bang Printing

10 9 8 7 6 5 4 3

All the Way to the Ocean

by Joel Harper · illustrated by Marq Spusta

foreword by Laird Hamilton

In loving memory of Dorothy Chase.

-J.H.

For all the critters.

- M.S.

A Statement from the Author

Some of my fondest childhood memories are those of sitting on the beach at twilight with my family. My brothers and I loved to watch the sand crabs dig their way home into the sand as the tide rolled back into the sea. I remember scooping up handfuls of sand and asking my mother, "Mom, are there more pieces of sand at the beach or stars in the sky?" Her answer fascinated me. "I think there are more stars in the sky."

I also remember seeing warning signs above the storm drains at the beach during my family outings. Now, although I live many miles from the ocean, they are posted in my hometown. The signs in my community have a blue fish inside a circle and lettering that says NO DUMPING—THIS DRAINS TO OCEAN. Depending on where you live, these signs may look a bit different.

It pains me that, despite the warning signs, our society has been careless in protecting the earth's oceans, rivers and lakes that we all depend on and love. People, plants, and sea creatures are getting sick from the pollution draining into our oceans. I am hopeful that we will change the tide and that *All the Way to the Ocean* may serve as a gentle reminder that, by working together, we can preserve these natural resources and ensure they will be here for future generations.

Joel Harper

Foreword

I am passionate about the ocean—riding her waves, swimming in her waters, exploring her floors and trying to find ways to take care of her. It is important for young people to be educated about how this system of nature works. *All the Way to the Ocean* is an opportunity to learn about how our actions link directly back to nature. Collectively and individually, we have a great responsibility to protect the ocean and the wonderful creatures that live there. If we all do just a little, together we can give a lot. It's not just fish and turtles that call the sea home; she is home to all of us. In Hawaii, there is a belief that you receive Mana (power) from nature. If you take care of nature, then nature can give you good Mana.

The ocean is a gift for all of us to enjoy and she should be cherished.

Mahalo nui loa—
(Thank you very much)

Laird Hamilton

Every day Isaac and his best friend, James, ride
their skateboards home from school.

"Should we hang out at your house or mine?" asked Isaac.

"Let's go to my house. My mom went shopping
and bought lots of good food," said James.

"Want a piece of candy?"

"Sure," said James.

"Hey, what are you doing?" asked Isaac.

"Did you just drop your wrapper into the storm drain?"

"Yeah, what's the big deal?" asked James.

"It's a big deal because these drains go all the way to the ocean, just like the sign says."

"What do you think happens when our trash ends up in the ocean?" asked Isaac.

"I don't know, what?" asked James.

"The plants and animals get really sick, that's what!"

"Look at all that trash that's already in there!" cried Isaac. "Plastic bags, cigarette butts, broken glass, bottle caps, plastic soda can holders and now your candy wrapper. There's even an old shoe down there!

"And guess what? As soon as it rains, all that trash goes straight to the ocean."

"How do you know?" asked James.

"'Cause I read about it in *National Geographic Kids*."

"Are you sure that stuff goes all the way to the ocean?" asked James.

"I'm positive!" said Isaac.

"Let's ask my mom when we get home. She's super smart."

"She's not smarter than *National Geographic*," said Isaac.

"Yes, she is," insisted James.

"Hey, mom, do the storm drains around town go all the way to the ocean?" asked James.

"They sure do," she replied.

"I told you!" said Isaac.

"Why do you ask, honey?"

Isaac jumped in and said, "Because James threw trash in the storm drain on the way home from school. He didn't know that they drain all the way to the ocean."

"Isaac is right about the storm drains," said James' mother. "Just think about all the harmful things that could happen when our trash ends up in the ocean!"

"All kinds of marine life are getting sick and their homes are becoming polluted. Sometimes they get stuck in our garbage."

"Do all storm drains go to the ocean?" asked James.

"Yes, they do," said his mother. "That's why it is important to remember not to throw trash on the ground. Because when it rains, harmful pollutants like foam cups, fast food wrappers, motor oil and even pet waste wash into storm drains and run down to lakes, rivers and the ocean."

"I saw someone reach out of their car and dump out their entire ashtray, full of cigarette butts, into the gutter by school one day," said James.

"I bet a lot of them ended up in the ocean."

"You're right, Isaac," said James' mother.

"Fish and birds often mistake cigarette butts and many other kinds of garbage for food. When they eat them they get sick.

"Sometimes sea turtles will eat plastic bags, thinking they're jellyfish! Jellyfish make a great lunch for a sea turtle, but plastic bags don't."

"Mom, can our drinking water get polluted, too?" asked James.

"Yes, it sure can, James. Runoff from storm drains can harm drinking water and affect recreational areas. Sometimes beaches have to be closed because the water is too dirty to swim in."

"Yeah, I know!" said Isaac. "My brother was mad last weekend 'cause he couldn't go surfing at his favorite spot. He said the beach was closed because of pollution."

"Pollution sure causes a lot of problems. Why do people litter so much?"

"That's a good question, Isaac. Maybe some people aren't aware of the harmful effects pollution has on the environment, or maybe they think that the ocean is so big that it has room for our trash. Sadly, that's not true. The ocean has more life in it than any other ecosystem on earth and we need to take better care of it," said James' mother.

"Hey, Isaac, you know all those gutters by school?" asked James.

"Yeah," said Isaac.

"I always see trash in them. Let's ask our teacher if our class can pick up trash around the school so it doesn't end up in the storm drains!" said James.

"Good idea! Maybe the whole school can pitch in. There's a lot of trash," said Isaac.

James and Isaac's teacher thought a schoolyard cleanup was a great idea.

After their classmates learned about storm drain pollution, they wanted to help clean up their environment. Many of the students even picked up garbage around their own neighborhoods.

What are some of the things you and your friends and family can do in your community to help prevent storm drain pollution?

About the Save Our Seas Foundation

There are many people and organizations working worldwide to protect and preserve our oceans and the inhabitants that live within. The Save Our Seas Foundation is one such organization that we support. Please read their mission statement on the following page and log on to learn more about Save Our Seas: You will discover ways in which you can become involved in protecting the world's oceans, lakes and rivers. We encourage you to become aware of what you can do both in your neighborhood and as part of a global community that works to protect these vital natural resources. No effort is too small to make a difference.

"Through the creation of Save Our Seas Foundation, I want to give all people an awareness of the importance and beauty of the ocean. I want to make our earth a healthier place by helping to preserve the ocean world I have come to love and respect so much. As long as there are people who care and take action we can and will make a difference." *–The Founder, Save Our Seas Foundation*

For more information on how to help protect the world's oceans, lakes and rivers, please visit:

SaveOurSeas.com
SOSforKids.com
SOSforTeens.com
AlltheWaytotheOcean.com

Mission Statement

save our seas
FOUNDATION

Save Our Seas Foundation is a non-profit organization headquartered in Geneva, Switzerland. Its purpose is to implement and support diverse programs of education, protection and conservation in locations around the world. Recent estimates suggest that in the 1970s the earth lost one species per day but this may now have increased to as much as one species per hour. Scientists have proved that many marine creatures have survived millions of years—unchanged—in unforgiving, often hostile environments. Not until human interference came into play did this balance become seriously upset, affecting the plight of our marine life dramatically and, as a consequence, the future of humanity as a whole.

While marine experts, scientists and policy makers around the world gather in various locations to discuss the issues of sand-starved beaches, pollution running into the sea, smog-spewing container ships, exhaustive overfishing and the devastation of sharks worldwide, a new charity, Save Our Seas Foundation, has been launched to help change the tide.

Encouraging awareness, protection, preservation and conservation of the global marine environment through research and education is at the heart of the Foundation's mission. Inspiring people, especially children, to fall in love with the sea by providing informative and educational materials will help create a better understanding of the ocean world and the many challenges that affect its delicate ecosystem.

The future of our seas and oceans lies in our hands today. But it is also crucial that we encourage the children of the world to embrace their role as guardians of the water world of tomorrow.

Marine Research Facility
P.O. Box 10646
Jeddah, 21443
SAUDI ARABIA

Dubai Office
P.O. Box 43659, Office #516A
Union House Building, 5th Floor
Port Saeed Road, Dubai
UNITED ARAB EMIRATES

Headquarters
Save Our Seas Foundation
6 Rue Bellot 1206
Geneve, Switzerland
Email: Contact@SaveOurSeas.com
www.SaveOurSeas.com

SaveOurSeas.com

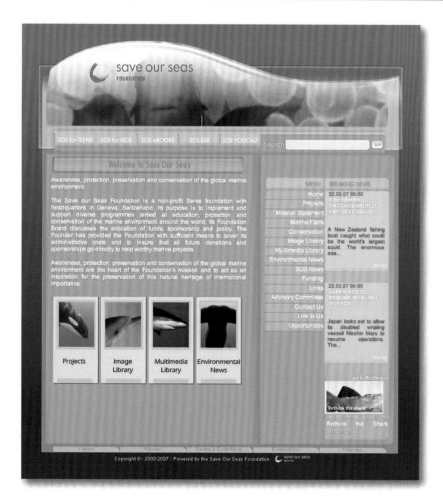

The Save Our Seas Foundation brings awareness, protection, preservation and conservation of the global marine environment. We are a non-profit Swiss foundation with headquarters in Geneva, Switzerland.

Its purpose is to implement and support diverse programs aimed at education, protection and conservation of the marine environment around the world. Its Foundation Board discusses the allocation of funds, sponsorship and policy. The Founder has provided the Foundation with sufficient means to cover its administrative costs and to insure that all future donations and sponsorships go directly to help worthy marine projects. Awareness, protection, preservation and conservation of the global marine environment are the heart of the Foundation's mission and to act as an inspiration for the preservation of this natural heritage of international importance.

If you would like more information about how to apply for funding for a project or simply wish to comment on our work and the website, you can write or email us at:

Save Our Seas Foundation (Switzerland)
Head Office
6 Rue Bellot, 1206 Geneva, Switzerland
Email: contact@saveourseas.com

SOSpodcast.com

For four years the Save Our Seas Foundation has been supporting over 30 projects in as many countries. From tagging White Sharks in South Africa to sponsoring pioneering research on the Manta Rays of Mexico and Mozambique, as well as producing a variety of educational training programmes and documentaries; the foundation is committed ensuring the preservation of our ocean realm for future generations.

This podcast series aims to showcase the work of the foundation and it's project leaders. The footage used has been gathered by the pioneering Save Our Seas film crew, who over the years, have produced one of the largest libraries of underwater High Definition stock footage in the world. Episode one highlights some of the issues currently surrounding marine conservation whilst the following episodes provide a more detailed insight into some of the marine species and projects that the foundation is involved with. *"As long as there are people who care and take action, we can and we will make a difference."*

Log on to www.SOSpodcast.com to experience this wondrous collection of underwater cinematography.

SOSforTeens.com

At SOSforTeens.com you can learn about marine life and what creatures lived in the ocean in the past and which ones are now living and swimming under the sea.

Do you know what an "Abyssopelagic Zone" is? Or, what a "Zooplankton" is? If not, you can go to SOSforTeens.com and check out the cool glossary section to learn all sorts of new Marine Biology terms.

What can you do to help and to conserve marine life?
You could work as a volunteer. This is rewarding and worthwhile, dedicating some time and effort to a local sea conservation group. You could participate in the clearing of coasts and beaches. Older students could also consider ´gap year´ options, where they could perhaps be accepted as a volunteer abroad, working with international projects such as sea turtles in Costa Rica. Perhaps you could learn how to dive and could then become a volunteer diver.

How you can get your community involved?
You can try to get your school, your local youth hostel or other local groups, involved in clean-up days, in parks, woodland areas, local beaches etc. By organizing events like these, you will attract local publicity and this is a great way of making everyone in your community much more aware of pollution and, of course, trying to prevent it.

SOSforKids.com

SOSesr.com

You can visit SOSforKids.com to play fun games, look at exciting ocean photos, through the photo album, view cool links, hear stories told by Nixie, "The Water Sprite" or Super Shark and do online colouring. You can also learn about the ocean and see what you can do to help preserve and protect it.

This Save Our Seas Educational Resources site has been designed to help teachers with planning, resources and ideas for teaching water related topics to nursery and infant aged children. Each teacher will decide the focus and depth of inquiry into a topic and can select activities to suit their needs. The "Report Creation" tool will create custom PDF files, which are printable. All reports are automatically saved for future reference. As a teacher, you need only to register, at no cost, to access our data-base of water-related activities, experiments and investigations.

All topic resources address key curriculum areas for elementary school children but of course, all activities are easily modifiable for slightly older children. There are planning aids, topic webs and educational points, all designed to help teachers provide stimulating and engaging topics.

save our seas
FOUNDATION